JACK THE STRIPPER
PAUL SUTTON

Newton-le-Willows

Published in the United Kingdom in 2021
by The Knives Forks And Spoons Press,
51 Pipit Avenue,
Newton-le-Willows,
Merseyside,
WA12 9RG.

ISBN 978-1-912211-77-7

Copyright © Paul Sutton, 2021.

The right of Paul Sutton to be identified as the author of this work has been asserted by them in accordance with the Copyrights, Designs and Patents Act of 1988. All rights reserved. No part of this publication may be reproduced, stored in a retrieval system, transmitted in any form or by any means, electronic, photocopying, recording or otherwise, without prior permission of the publisher.

Acknowledgements:

Some of these pieces first appeared in:

Stride; International Times; Anti-Heroin Chic; I am not a silent poet; Litter; Anthropocene.

Many thanks to their editors.

Contents

Prologue	7
A Man in Acton Wearing a Trilby	9
Woodlands	10
Dreaming About Money	11
Cities Built by Our First Murderers	12
Architectures of Childhood	13
Regeneration	14
Heaven Must Be Missing an Angel	15
Under Gas	16
St Catharine's College, Cambridge	17
Devaluation of Higher Education	18
Creative Writing Tutor	19
Founding Myths	20
His Story	22
In my Mother's House	28
Appraising the Magpie of Stonebridge Park	29
Psychiatric Evaluation	34
Gone Below	35
The Mystery of Skidmore Hall	36
Mud and Sun	44

JACK THE STRIPPER

PROLOGUE

Something he was always looking for,
counting coins in endless bars, a drink –
and he's away. London's wanderer, its
only true poet. Such hunters forge
the legends we hear, take us back to
wolves harrying Saxon homesteads,
men from the North Sea running boats
up pebbles, leaping ashore – then
all the madness and fire anyone can
bring. Maybe descended from Odin,
killer outcast, forced away to sail
the salt way, exiled – a nightmare
from our broken arcades or
boarded-up seafronts.

Jack the Stripper

A MAN IN ACTON WEARING A TRILBY

He doesn't say much now,
just dreams of dying – alone –
bones become burnt branches;
scorch-zones on towpaths
where he left naked bodies.

Any man can imagine this,
cars idling, the girls waiting.
'It would have been better
to get caught' – unlucky he
never was. Here's a thing to

tell his grandchildren: 'London
was the city that needed paying,
and I'm not the only one done
such things to make payment.
What's my worry? Nothing.'

I can't say he even enjoyed dusk.
On those roads which head west,
the sun often explodes then says:
'It's time to get moving, life slows,
starts to clump. Traffic never waits.'

Paul Sutton

WOODLANDS

I could feel nothing for months,
then as I drove down the M4 I'd
smell pine trees being felled and
wonder – why here – also how the
taste of wood in my nose takes me
back to those straggly bits of magic,
for hiding or growth – sudden loss.

So many woodlands – mostly untrodden –
no one knows who planted them. Navigate
new estates, school-fields, aggro-parks –
lonely poplars marching by pylons;
the code's in there somewhere.

The Unabomber played names –
anything good had splintered
him. Who hasn't seen a tall man
run across a road, hop a fence
then fall to the ground?

There's no evidence.
Single men summoning
infinite railway bridges,
numberless carparks.

Laws?

Yes, they give answers –
investigations.
When arrests are made
I can't be involved.

DREAMING ABOUT MONEY

It's the first time I have – an envelope,
a cheque for 19,800 – pounds – I was
being fired from a terrible job and my
friend was getting £200,010. God only
knows it was odd – but with a child, who
doesn't want more money? Well, the rich
obviously, though I've never been especially
poor (except for now). But it's terrible to
be ashamed of this – better to pretend,
spend, worry about it later. In dreams
you can't hide, you'll get caught –
wake up and try and not forget.

Paul Sutton

CITIES BUILT BY OUR FIRST MURDERERS

Surely they should all have fallen by now?
Children can look at fields, see them stretch
endless – no boundaries, though the place is
set for wrecking. Someone said that
the more fragile, the more beautiful:
the gentlest folds in England worth
numberless chasms, glowering peaks.
I'm glad to become philistine, don't care
if others' beauties get destroyed. What's
worse than hearing about souls – deader
than the dreams you tell to bore even
yourself. Just remember those long days,
how slowly the sun drops, backwards
into the vanished landscape you go.

ARCHITECTURES OF CHILDHOOD

Somehow, gravel pits are still exciting,
new-build estates, demantoid grass to
tape-crossed windows. Those reservoirs
we'd zip past and I'd dream of fishing
there – or sun-struck French towns –
the steep enclosed rivers – men with
those huge French fishing poles out
to glassy calm. Let's be honest, the
smell was vaguely sewage, but then
waking to hot chocolate and a VW
bus to the Brittany coast of Canvas
Holidays. I've also got poplar trees
from our back-garden's end – I love
the faded green and their restless
movement, so not climbable now,
or ever. It isn't size that changes
but too many unnecessary things,
they invade and push away the
foundations you don't see.

Paul Sutton

REGENERATION

About 1974, driving into London, my parents' car,
I'd be terrified of the houses, those north London
hulks then slums and blocks, worst of all when
there were curtains – or even shampoo bottles.
Who lived there, how did they manage, was
the food terrible – colours pastel and peeling.

I was warned about slums, how drinkers
drunk death, the rooms in black and white –
Don McCullin or Roger Mayne. Now that's
gone, vanished like Atlantis or Lyonesse.
Perhaps they needed someone to dig the
roads out – so much got left there.

To be honest, I don't think it matters;
my social history is vastly pointless.
I could share a million memories
and still walk through some town,
to worry about who uses buses
so late, where this traffic goes.

HEAVEN MUST BE MISSING AN ANGEL

I may be a miserable bastard,
but I've always loved this song;
somehow I don't even know who wrote it.
It's some 1970s scene, sun in the morning,
heatwave gathering strength and all of the
shops selling skateboards with wheels of
fruit juice colours. I wouldn't have got why
he was happy, though I may have noticed
hair or tits, tight bum on some girl called
Sharon Davies – it's animal, certainly not
cruel. Hearing it now, I can't believe the joy;
a man is making someone coffee and can
ignore almost everything to sing of angels –
it's beyond ridiculous, but sometimes that's
needed. It's played about once a month in
The Seacourt Bridge, my local. Last night,
I overheard a sad couple in discussion:
'My husband he sees everything in
black and white.' I looked over smiling –
bad move; I think she was nuts – she
asked me to join them, if I was 'that
interested'. I declined this kind offer,
explaining that I just like listening.

Paul Sutton

UNDER GAS

My grandfather's book on meteorology
starts gently, with him reminding us:
'We live under a sea of gas.'
He's gone now, of course –
some are crushed immediately,
some slowly – though they resist,
to feel the exhalations of centuries
bearing down. Others get spontaneous
combustion – which sounds comical,
but destroys soft furnishings,
sometimes houses.

ST CATHARINE'S COLLEGE, CAMBRIDGE

My father's closest friend was a fellow, in Spanish and South American literature.

His one aim in life was to ensure this connection yielded me a prestigious scholarship, at that most unattractive of Cambridge's ancient colleges.

We holidayed biannually with this acquaintance – a hairy and unhygienic dwarf – whose ears sprouted wandering tendrils of insane seaweed.

Dr Rodriquez made frequent attempts to seduce me – claiming an affinity with the Apostles, and E.M. Forster.

At last, I was invited for interview.

My interlocutor was a complete stranger.

Since I spoke not a word of Spanish – and had never heard of Pablo Neruda – I was violently escorted from the premises.

Kidneys jabbed, my head locked – testicles under bombardment – I glanced into the Porter's Lodge and saw Rodriquez, reading *One Hundred Years of Solitude*.

Paul Sutton

DEVALUATION OF HIGHER EDUCATION

Quite unexpectedly, I met Rodriquez many years later.

My father severed their intense – yet ultimately fruitless – relationship.

He then shrank alarmingly – eventually living in a matchbox.

I was forced to work my passage 'before the mast', to South America.

That vast continent, rivers running in mud and loot, so suited to a young man out for his fortune.

I returned to England as a pauper – arriving in Tilbury with the Fray Bentos pies and petrified bird shit.

Rodriquez met me off the ship, proffering a copy of Conrad's impenetrable novel *Nostromo*.

CREATIVE WRITING TUTOR

For years, I chronicled our motorway service stations.

It was enough to see sunset over the slip-roads, sunrise over burgeoning budget hotels, snow falling onto university technology colleges.

An insomniac army marched with me – miles from urban elites and their innumerable allergies.

Literature had vanished, but the causes grew.

When someone dies, and then years pass, where are they all that time?

Now I come to write about it all, my experiences are trivial but unstoppable.

Paul Sutton

FOUNDING MYTHS

Although a working-class lad – my father a Derbyshire glue-miner, mother a sock fitter – I rose to prominence at Oxford, eventually joining the Bullingdon Club.

I was merciless in my exploits.

My inner knowledge allowed me to sniff out members of the lower orders – many were exterminated in gravel pits, at Radley.

You may think this tasteless, but my intentions were hilarity.

Especially beloved were newly-opened restaurants, where pitiful owners 'sunk life-savings' into dreams of regeneration with food fit for *The Guardian*.

We'd dress as Congolese nuns, enquiring if an annual prayer meeting could be held there – offering extraordinary largesse.

Needless to say, the place would be obliterated.

People are extraordinarily tolerant of privilege – many thanked us for utterly destroying their dreams.

Have you been in a housing estate, on Christmas Eve?

The lights twinkling and the sound of broken bones?

If you have, such frippery can be excused.

You see, there must be a moral.

In many ways, I regret those days.

Jack the Stripper

I see a huge metaphor working its way outwards.

Now I plan caravans and stress-free retreats.

Weep at road-kills, horses in winter coats.

Please remember, everyone gets hurt.

Paul Sutton

HIS STORY

I.

A vague memory
of being an expert –
in what, he couldn't say.

Someone who didn't stare
at fields, grey torn pages,
adults with dirty secrets.

He wrote complicated
volumes – remembers
just this:

'As written, nothing makes sense. I know what it means;
lost time and strength show I can't hope to speak truth.'

A murder story – detectives planning the killings.

Political cover, social status, full cupboards –
everything needed for a life of crime.

Voting makes no difference. Once there were countries, but they stopped
efficient leisure, movement of slaves, poisoned meats.

All that's left are stamp albums, with golds and purples, chocolate names.

Workers in dying areas – who once made the volumes – thrown into
gravel pits, forced to crawl up pylons.

Few understood the crimes.

Jack the Stripper

After solving those, he was
praised, promoted, awarded
every literary prize – adapted
by the BBC – then invited to
fornicate with a pub fireplace
or plunge down to an ocean's
bed and await the wreckage.

On the surface, with binoculars,
exhausting bird-watching optics,
the approaching cliffs are combed
in microscopic detail.

No one onboard seems worried.

But they loom higher –
the sight is gorgeous –
every gemstone glittering,
every species desporting itself
in full extinction glory.

Paul Sutton

II.

It's always the same, your Utopian dreams;
golden wings flying to crystalized horizons.
Here's a multi-storey carpark, old urine,
many a child dragged from a car into one
of the shoe shops – the mother now dead –
you can't forget how those early shopping
centres seemed magical – overheated – even
old people dropping to their knees and crying
at the plenitude. Home to see Dad's war films,
their theme tunes whistled by an entire street –
utter nonsense – but the lack of deadening
variety was a strength – fantastic to have
bad pubs, no indoctrination of perfection.

In Russian literature, you sit in a room
so many years later, remember an angel
you failed to sleep with – the one who
eloped with her private tutor then got
ravished by seven drunken serfs. This
doesn't work in Stevenage, Hatfield or
Welwyn Garden City. For starters, there
aren't spaces left on the map – no canals,
no sempiternal mists to hide lurkers plus
our culture wouldn't allow us. Laughing
at bad dinners and dictatorial women in
purple irradiated dresses – teeth which
drag all the air away – that's England.

I must admit, I followed her home
the first time she walked back alone –
it was my daughter – I could have
cried at her serious look, checking
each road, every car, looking straight
ahead, refusing even to talk to some
friends she passed. There's nothing

Jack the Stripper

better than simplicity, the moment
the complexity dies away to show
structure and meaning. You can't hold
it though, thank goodness – its fading
is the purpose. How you love never
lasts, somehow another way arrives.

III.

It has to be admitted, I was hellishly unpopular, at both school and 'the university'.

My presence caused constant outrage.

Petitions, demonstrations – and outbreaks of violence in my vicinity – convince me I was a menace, to myself and the wider 'community'.

At school there was a timed event to see who could escape my company the fastest.

A complicated system of semaphore messaging – organised by the science masters – signalled my imminent arrival.

Competitors on the starting line awaited the first sight of my flared trousers and flapping tie.

AWAY!

I remained oblivious – imagining myself the school's only pupil.

Only at Prize Day – when I entered the hall and triggered a calamitous rush for the exits, causing several deaths – did the truth strike me.

I arrived at the university forewarned, to little avail.

The authorities systematically razed buildings to the ground whenever I dared stroll its delightful streets.

A scene worthy of the Blitz met my weary steps – gothic splendours, venerable bridges and tremulous towers, collapsing round me.

Even 'Professors of Geography' were dismayed, though thankful their despised subject now assumed some importance.

Luckily, I was refused an academic career – on the grounds that tenure would be fatal.

IV.

People from the past, kicking at my heart.
Lions in multiple story car parks, they
roar in solitude – then rip me apart.
So much beauty, far deadlier than none.
Mismatching that within – boiling over.
Everything as a child seems unearned.
I never thought it was for those beyond
any thanks, for them to get joy in mine.

Paul Sutton
IN MY MOTHER'S HOUSE

The worst thing with her dementia
is all these emotions have gone –
no anger, nothing left of the fire.

I remember one winter in Welwyn
Garden City, somehow she got
involved in deliveries to families
where the father was in prison –
children in dirty vests at the door –
bread and jam on Christmas Eve.

Dickensian – I guess it sounds a cliché.
She was in tears and couldn't explain.
Driving home in silence, no blame for
us, just mute. This was a Utopian new
town, not rich, the poorer parts were
shunned, lost fifties council houses by
factories where shredded wheat was made –
I imagined the people living in them
eating cereal and nothing else. Now
shredded wheat itself seems a horror,
like old hair or straw from a scarecrow.

She was from a bone-poor family of
Smyrna Greek refugees I didn't
understand; said she'd slept in
shipping crates and had to buy
her own Christmas presents –
told to get herself something.

APPRAISING THE MAGPIE OF STONEBRIDGE PARK

I. A lead

I am a crime writer.

Seemingly unsuccessful – my books cannot even be found in garden centres.

I need a lead.

Elderly puffins – Ted and Ruthie – timeshared in the '80s, reduced to muttering in our local, between weeks in Bulgaria.

An opening.

They tell of a bronzed villain – carved like amber – who stripped them of coin and sung like a magpie.

'A nightingale?'

'A scrapyard magpie!'

Nightly his victims – aware they 'share a cubicle in a Tenerife shit-house' – endured his descanting, counting their diminishing cash.

Now they have an address.

A huge breaker washed this legend away from his Deptford manor, to the worst estate in London – north of the river, north of anywhere (except gun crime).

Even the UN have withdrawn their troops, after an incident with a Swedish peacekeeper and an obese mother of sixteen in a condemned chicken outlet.

The man was deep fried then served on chutty bread.

His family received a pair of trainers and a flyer for pizza delivery.

Like a Poundland Buddha, I found Terry Palmer on his balcony, singing for the encircling youths:

'Poppadoms ain't no good for a fry-up ... ghee gets in your eyes ... the silver off the streets and a Terry's chocolate orange sunset ... a bunk-up with some black bird ... oh Mogadishu's where me love is ... the councillors give planning permission ... refugee camps in Victorian gardens ... I used a blade ... now we got Khan who can't ... too much aftershave at Heathrow ... one day these boys will get me bent over a bike rack ... a stairwell roistering ... we'll revenge ... Olaf the Swede ... skin white as Mother's Pride ... that works for a fry-up ... oh Kosovo my dinkum ... Serbs may carve but I love you ... Simon Armitage has my back ... he can write about goalies who smoke ... northern pies ... give me eels and batter ... Buckfast for the Sweaties ... little girls skipping in the early mist ... one village I saw on the Weald ... now a lorry-park.' ...

II. An overrated horror film

None of it usable –
mostly unprintable:
all of it 'offensive'.

I remember that cult horror film,
fire burning, a man in the middle,
'singing for his supper.'

III. Appraisal

I now work in the public-sector, valuing diversity and ensuring equality of opinion and outcome.

This requires listening skills – covertly – then enforcement of managerial sanctions on reactionary elements.

Unconscious bias is our greatest enemy.

Often at night, in the distracting hum from ring-roads, creeping into children's bedrooms, filling their dreams with global or historical pollutants.

By day, it digs away until attitudes suited to Kristallnacht are heard in birdsong, or squeals from the playground.

Recently, I have doubted my own purity.

On local buses sit numerous foreigners (often highly decorated) alongside obvious lavender-wearers, prowling for 'contacts'.

I welcome such vibrancy, but sometimes wonder what difference an old-fashioned Tommy gun fired in the face would make to their confidence.

I write with no worry these harmless words will be misquoted, nor my obvious humour misunderstood.

Hatred is everywhere.

It calls to us persistently, like those insistent rooks now disturbing my typing.

Nothing emerges from our howling meetings, psychotic PowerPoints and deathly appraisals – save unread paperwork, defaced with the deformed genitals I sketch anonymously, hoping to get caught.

In more progressive cultures, I would be paraded around a stadium – wearing a sign detailing my crime – then shot for the enlightened masses.

* * * * *

Of course, the rain was the same when I was a child – but it tastes different now.

Imagine an educated man, alone, in some socialist paradise.

The tower blocks, the parks, the clean lines straight out to an industrial zone of power against the endless steppe.

Well, that's not me.

But I hear them circling.

Not corvids, but the managerial dictators of who does what, where.

Oh you can run as a child, perhaps scrape your shin.

You don't imagine men laid like meat on slabs, cells bursting one by one.

Have I started to smell?

Decay is our lot – and in some way to be welcomed.

IV. Psychiatric evaluation (by senior management)

Reviewing these notes, it seems incredible the writer wasn't apprehended sooner.

This reinforces the need for more invasive and comprehensive monitoring.

Those responsible for such negligence need disciplining.

There is no thought but the one thought –

which has already been done for us.

GONE BELOW

Now it's all gone, I could sit
on some mountain forever,
not thinking about moving or

worrying when the bar closed,
how long the holiday lasted,
just existing up there.

Everything would return:
family, childhood, stuff
you want to remember.

And that one place would've
waited many centuries for me,
certain someday I'd go back.

I'll not say a word, just travel,
ignoring the airports and mad
pathogens – maybe up within

the coldest clouds, above
the wreckage littering
what's here below.

All the years you hated me,
when I must have hated you.
Gardens, houses, meetings –

impossible to chart – now
this poison floods the past
we had. I can't think how

I feel – a nothing, that's always
there, not an absence and not
even a loss – just gone and lost.

Paul Sutton

THE MYSTERY OF SKIDMORE HALL

Of all the adventures I shared with my friend Sherlock Holmes, few fill my dreams with such horror as the events at Skidmore, Shropshire, in late November 1886. My experiences of the Afghan campaign had hardened me to much that is unsavoury, but I was left both shattered and weakened by our experiences in that ungodly border-country. Only now, with the recent demise of the last actor in this dismal story, can I reveal the truth behind our sudden departure from England, in early December of that year.

It was a gloomy evening of late autumn. Holmes – much exhausted by his recent unmasking of the Boston Butcher – lay in an apparent trance. Long acquainted with my friend's methods, I was not surprised when my reading was peremptorily interrupted.

'Events suggest a Study in Brown, Watson. Make of this what you will!'

He handed over a telegram, dated that same afternoon.

Come immediately, events of the utmost delicacy, urgent assistance required. Brownsword.

'Lord Brownsword is the scion of one of our greatest families,' I remarked. 'His residence at Skidmore Hall the very pride of the Marches, renovated at prodigious expense with the latest conveniences.'

'Indeed. His Lordship is a man whose curtness of manner is matched inversely with his vastness of fortune.' Holmes had already retrieved his much battered copy of Bradshaw's guide. 'We can take a fast train at 9:10, from Euston?'

My few commitments being then at a low ebb, I agreed immediately.

Next morning, an early breakfast and a rapid two-seater saw us leaving Euston and heading north, through London's dreary suburbs. Holmes occupied his time in perusal of a monograph on the efficacy of various rapidly ingested metallic poisons.

It soon became apparent that his research was not merely of a theoretical nature. On passing Kettering, a sour and spreading aroma indicated that Holmes had filled our compartment with arse-vapour. I fear my consciousness was soon lost, and awoke to find my companion's anxious face peering into mine.

'My dear Watson, I shall never forgive myself. I had no idea the cadmium I laced both our breakfasts with acted so quickly. May God have mercy on poor Mrs. Hudson's movements!'

The rest of the journey passed in a miasma of volcanic eruptions and scribbled notes – Holmes meticulously noting the frequency and forcefulness of our embarrassments. It was only with difficulty that I dissuaded him from attempting 'flame testing', with a lighted taper. A disastrous experience during the siege of Peshawar, suffered by a junior subaltern after an excess of Camel Pathia, had alerted me to the terrible risk of 'blow-back' and buttock scorching.

It was with some relief that our journey ended, the Shropshire hills and dripping woodlands announcing our arrival at the isolated rural station of Skidmore Halt.

A groom awaited, and we were whisked away. The cold country air soon cleared my head and I watched with interest, as our carriage entered the splendid gates of Skidmore Hall. The house was originally Tudor, but had been so thoroughly 'Gothicised' as to seem a more recent construction. Of particular note were the many down pipes, somewhat disfiguring its elegant façade.

'His Lordship takes great pride in the provision of individual water closets for all his guests,' remarked Holmes, following my glance.

'Of no small relief to us both, you can be sure,' I replied, with some asperity. Although my bottom had achieved some temporary respite, I could only imagine what my first evacuation would involve. Holmes nodded, a smirk on his hawk-like features the only indication he heard my testy words.

To my surprise, Lord Brownsword awaited us in his entrance hall. A more unprepossessing example of the English aristocracy it would be hard to imagine. At first glance, he resembled a minor accounts clerk or draper's assistant. An unmistakable gravy stain was visible on his tweed jacket and the faint aroma of old cabbages – or even Jerusalem artichoke – lingered around him.

'Gentlemen, you catch me on the hop,' he muttered, signalling for us to follow him up the grand double staircase. His movements gathered pace into a headlong charge, as he rushed for the nearest privy door.

We awaited his return in silence. I noted the ascending portraits of his departed ancestors, each a stepwise, atavistic return to the brutal reality of baronial squat toilets over castle walls. Holmes was clearly impatient. The Duke emerged and ushered us into an enormous upper hall, entirely papered in brown.

'If your Lordship would furnish us with all the details. Omit nothing, however seemingly trivial,' my friend instructed.

'Mr. Holmes. I have heard good report of both your discretion and your indefatigability.'

Holmes nodded his approval, encouraging the Duke to continue.

'You see around you a monument to English scatological emancipation. I am a well-read man, despite my somewhat insignificant appearance. For generations, the Brownswords have been cursed by lavatorial misfortune. And still, in all my studies, I have yet to encounter any other great family so similarly troubled.'

'Blockages?' I hazarded to suggest.

'If that were the problem, Dr. Watson, I would scarcely have inconvenienced so busy a man as Mr. Sherlock Holmes!' he replied. 'No, we face a more deadly and persistent terror.'

'Pray continue,' encouraged Holmes.

'I am a light sleeper, Mr. Holmes. The house, as you no doubt saw, is in the traditional 'H' shape, with four wings and this connecting gallery. There are in total, two dozen chambers, each with an ensuite Armitage Shanks.'

'Your Lordship is most gracious,' I assented.

Somewhat confused, Lord Brownsword continued. 'For the last two weeks, I have been awakened by persistent flushing noises. On entering each chamber, and proceeding to the convenience, I have found … marks.'

'Marks?' enquired Holmes.

'Mr. Holmes, they were the skid marks of an enormous turd!'

My friend tilted back his head and church-steepled his narrow fingers.

'To what degree – a one, two or three striper?'

Brownsword produced a crumpled paper, which he handed to my friend. It was clearly a tabulation, of dates, toilet locations and associated 'skid widths'.

'This appears to be in some sort of code,' Holmes muttered. 'I will need time to study it, over a number of pipes.'

'I am in your hands, Mr. Holmes,' replied the diminutive Duke.

'If your man could show us to our rooms, I can then report back to you after dinner.'

'Excellent. I have asked Mrs. Fisher to prepare us one of her mystery meat feasts. We dine at eight – dress is casual.'

With that he was gone. The gaunt figure of Jeyes, the butler, escorted us through the gallery.

'Holmes, what do you make of it?' I remarked, in utter confusion.

'There are dark things at work here, Watson. And yet I see a glimmer, a sign that the four-ply paper is not yet finished.'

'Gods preserve us from the Izal! But I still confess to utter bafflement.'

'You noticed the Duke's saddle-sore walk?'

'A keen huntsman, no doubt.'

'Arse-grapes, more likely. A hereditary curse of long-standing. The third Duke missed the Battle of Waterloo, thanks to them. His late father had to be carried into the House of Lords, grimacing on a raised dais of duck feathers.'

Holmes issued one of his mirthless laughs and was gone.

* * * * *

Dinner was a gloomy affair, partaken in the semi-darkness of the Great Hall. To my astonishment, we were served from what can only be described as a 'hygiene wagon', wheeled from end to end of the table by a Marigold-gloved Mrs. Fisher.

The food was quite inedible and, as course after course appeared, I resorted to throwing it under my chair. His Lordship ate both heartily and messily, interrupting his mastication to discourse on the Hall's elaborate plumbing work.

'A quite extraordinarily fascinating history, flushed away daily, but revealing man at his most basic.'

'Quite so,' agreed Holmes. 'When one considers how disgusting the average Englishman is – dragged down the centuries through wild boar, goose and pig shit – the beacon light of scientific advance blasting away this messy matter is the Fiat Lux of our day.'

'And yet all is now lost,' our host wailed.

'Have courage, my Lord. Approached through the lens of reason and deduction, even a thousand skid marks can never win.'

Later, over brandy and cigars, Holmes elaborated his findings.

'I commend our host on his rational approach to the matter. Many a lesser man would have taken fright and ignored the data on which our case will rest.'

'Holmes!' I ejaculated, 'You mean the identity of the Skidmore Hall skidder is known to you?'

'All in good time, Watson. I have my suspicions, but a night's observation – in the presence of yourself and your trusty service revolver – should bring matters to a head.'

Brownsword's features showed a momentary twitch of anxiety.

'Do I understand you intend to tackle this faecal fiend?'

Holmes turned his aquiline features in profile and stared into the falling embers. 'Watson and I have many years' experience of nocturnal reconnaissance. This is the last night on which your porcelain will be subjected to cable laying or giant otter attacks.'

He left the room.

* * * * *

A freezing vigil in the upper gallery was punctuated by those nightly disturbances encountered in England's grandest residences. From somewhere came the persistent scratching of mice in the wainscot. The wind shot its gusty fingers down numerous chimneys. Outside, a screech owl patrolled the vast lawns.

His Lordship's room was obvious from a cacophony of snoring and fevered tossing, audible even from our position, crouched behind a suit of medieval armour.

At just past 4am, Holmes touched my shoulder.

At first all was indistinct, but in the gloom I saw a faint procession of two-dozen masked figures, ascending the grand staircase. The lead figure was holding aloft an enormous stiff-haired toilet brush, like some monstrous perversion of the holy cross. A dull chanting, almost a liturgical drone, steadily increased in intensity as the procession made for the first chamber.

'Quick Watson. Not a second to lose.'

Holmes leapt into the fray. A pandemonium of toilet duck spraying and urinal cake throwing ensued. As we fought our way through to the first chamber door, I saw a dark shape emerging.

'My God, Holmes, the Skidder of Skidmore Hall!'

'We have it Watson!' My friend grabbed the toilet brush, and proceeded to smash the fleeting shadow. To my horror, pure excrement flew everywhere, pebble dashing us both and liberally coating our surroundings.

What were we facing? A creature of some dozen feet in length, topped with piercing yellow eyes (I later discovered these to be pieces of sweet-corn). Over the centuries, this monstrous turd had inhabited the pipework, emerging only at night to leave its distinctive markings in the Hall privies and terrify the constipated occupants.

With a final agonized sigh, alike to nothing so much as an enormous fart, the creature subsided and died.

By this time, our host was awake.

'Mr. Holmes! What is the meaning of this?'

'I had rather hoped you could explain that,' drawled Holmes.

The Duke was dressed in what appeared to be a monk's habit, with a headdress made from Izal toilet tissue.

Slumping onto the stairs, he revealed the sorry history behind these outrageous events.

'It can little profit me to hide the truth. This matter stretches back, like some grotesque faecal tape worm, to the fourth Duke's disgrace. As Dr. Watson can testify, many an Englishman has returned from our Indian possessions with a liking for curry.'

'Indeed,' I averred, 'My own weakness was for a Chicken Karachi!'

'The fourth Duke took his fondness to extremes – kidnapping the entire catering staff from the Maharaja of Jalfrezi. In so doing, he brought down – on himself and his unfortunate successors – the Holy Brahim's Curse of the Curried Arse.'

'I feared as much,' muttered Holmes. 'Indeed, the code you handed me was an ancient Sanskrit text, promising anal agony for any who insulted the honour of the Jalfrezi family.'

'On returning to England, my ancestor was plagued by a near biblical infestation of winnuts, tag nuts and dangle berries. The more furiously he wiped, the more persistently his arsehole was attacked by these monstrous blighters.'

'Until the Duke expired, after laying this enormous coiler we see before us.' completed Holmes. 'And since that day, it bided its time, alive in the growing plumbing installed by successive generations of Brownswords.'

The three of us looked in horror, at the ruin of this once great estate. The Duke explained how this foul creature had demanded nightly penance, with his loyal staff deputed to clean the terrific skid marks left on its nocturnal visits.

Holmes and I had removed the curse, but at what cost to this great house? We departed the next morning, amidst futile attempts to employ the latest steam cleaning and sand blasting techniques. A sickly brown cloud seemed to hang over Skidmore Hall as we took our leave.

On our return to London, we received news that the Duke had set his ancestral home alight and moved into a council flat, in nearby Telford New Town. The ensuing scandal – with questions in the House and virulent press attacks on Holmes – led us to our current retreat, amidst the unchanging splendours of the Upper Nile.

Paul Sutton

MUD AND SUN

Sudden sunlight hits the road
as you drive past what you've known –
seen in the rear-view – then gone.
We understand these don't last
but what matters isn't this.

Winds open the fields to trees.
Long hills crest the horizon.
Somehow a child sees a horse
carved into chalk, then riding,
riding out over estates,

long days, paths of joy, new towns
where forgotten rivers flow
over boots, the children's toes
washed in purest mud which cleans
everything – leaving me this.

Titles by Paul Sutton

Broadsheet Asphyxia (Original Plus, collection, 2003).

The Chronicles of Dave Turnip (Original Plus, pamphlet, 2009).

Brains Scream at Night (BlazeVOX books, collection, 2010).

Voiceover (with Rupert Loydell, The Knives, Forks and Spoons Press, pamphlet, 2011).

Indigo not Violet (The Red Ceilings Press, e-book, 2011).

Gemstones (The Red Ceilings Press, pamphlet, 2011).

Cabin Fever (The Knives, Forks and Spoons Press, collection, 2012).

The Turnip's Return (The Red Ceilings Press, e-book, 2013).

Encouraging Signs (Shearsman, essays and interviews by Rupert Loydell; detailed interview on Sutton's poetry and poetics, 2013).

Falling Off (The Knives, Forks and Spoons Press, collection, 2015 - Poetry Book Society Recommended Reading, for Autumn 2015).

Taxi Drivers (The Red Ceilings Press, pamphlet, 2016).

To Say (Smallminded Books, pamphlet, 2016)

The Diversification of Dave Turnip (The Knives, Forks and Spoons Press, collection, 2017).

The Sorry History of Fast Food (Leafe Press, pamphlet, 2017).

Parables for the Pouring Rain (BlazeVOX books, collection, 2018).

Jack the Stripper (The Knives, Forks and Spoons Press, collection, 2021).

www.ingramcontent.com/pod-product-compliance
Lightning Source LLC
Chambersburg PA
CBHW011309060426
42444CB00040B/3456